A Note to Parents

DK READERS is a compelling program for beginning readers, designed in conjunction with leading literacy experts, including Dr. Linda Gambrell, Professor of Education at Clemson University. Dr. Gambrell has served as President of the National Reading Conference and the College Reading Association, and has recently been elected to serve as President of the International Reading Association.

Beautiful illustrations and superb full-color photographs combine with engaging, easy-to-read stories to offer a fresh approach to each subject in the series. Each DK READER is guaranteed to capture a child's interest while developing his or her reading skills, general knowledge, and love of reading.

The five levels of DK READERS are aimed at different reading abilities, enabling you to choose the books that are exactly right for your child:

Pre-level 1: Learning to read
Level 1: Beginning to read
Level 2: Beginning to read alone
Level 3: Reading alone
Level 4: Proficient readers

The "normal" age at which a child begins to read can be anywhere from three to eight years old, so these levels are only a general guideline.

No matter which level you select, you can be sure that you are helping your child learn to read, then read to learn!

LONDON, NEW YORK, MUNICH,
MELBOURNE, and DELHI

Series Editor Penny Smith
Senior Art Editor Sonia Moore
U.S. Editors Elizabeth Hester,
John Searcy
U.S. Dental Consultant
Lois A. Jackson, D.D.S.
DTP Designer Almudena Díaz
Production Angela Graef
Picture Research Rose Horridge
Photography Andy Crawford

Reading Consultant
Linda Gambrell, Ph.D.

First American Edition, 2006
06 07 08 09 10 10 9 8 7 6 5 4 3 2 1
Published in the United States by DK Publishing, Inc.
375 Hudson Street, New York, New York 10014

DK books are available at special discounts for bulk purchases for sale
promotions, premiums, fundraising, or educational use. For details, contact:
DK Publishing Special Markets
375 Hudson Street
New York, New York 10014
SpecialSales@dk.com

Library of Congress Cataloging-in-Publication Data
Smith, Penny.
A trip to the dentist / written by Penny Smith.-- 1st American ed.
p. cm. -- (DK readers. Level 1, beginning to read)
ISBN-13 978-0-7566-1914-5 ISBN-10 0-7566-1914-9 (paperback)
ISBN-13 978-0-7566-1915-2 ISBN 0-7566-1915-7 (hardcover)
1. Dentistry--Juvenile literature. 2. Children--Preparation for dental care-
-Juvenile literature. I. Title. II. Series: Dorling Kindersley readers.
1. Beginning to read
RK63.S569 2006
617.6--dc22
                                                                    2005032705

Color reproduction by Colourscan, Singapore
Printed and bound in China by L Rex Printing Co., Ltd.

With thanks to: The Hill View Dental Practice, Harrow, London,
for premises and staff appearing in the photographs; Cameron and Nikhita
Jackson and their mother Geeta Nanda for appearing in the photographs.
Alexander Workwear, London, for dental coats; LydiaUniforms.com for
dental scrubs; OpenWide.com for dental accessories.
All images © Dorling Kindersley
For more information see: www.dkimages.com

Discover more at

www.dk.com

DK READERS

BEGINNING
1
TO READ

A Trip to the Dentist

Written by Penny Smith

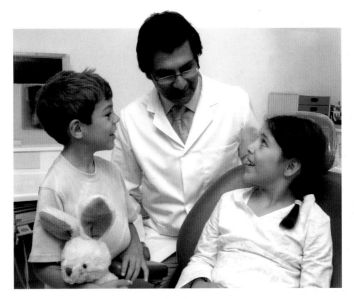

DK Publishing, Inc.

"Come on, get your coats," called Mom.
Sarah and her brother, Josh, tumbled into the room.

"It's time to go
to the dentist
for your checkups,"
said Mom.

Soon they arrived at
the dentist's office.
Mom told the receptionist
their names.

"I want my teeth
to stay strong and
white like Rabbit's,"
Josh told her.

rabbit

The children played in the
waiting room until it was time
for their checkups.

Then the dentist
took them into the
examination room.
"Hi," he said.
"My name is Dr. Richards."

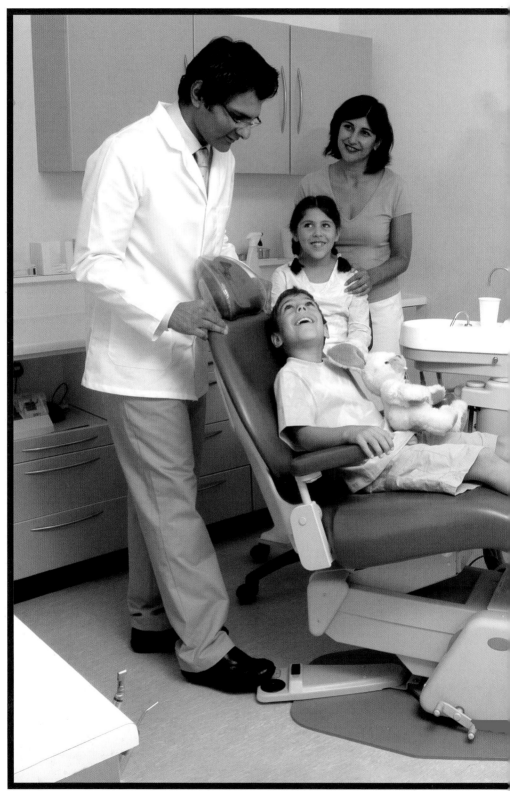

"Who's going first?"
asked Dr. Richards.
Josh climbed into the chair
with Rabbit.
The dentist pressed a button
and the chair tipped
slowly backward.

dentist

"Open wide," said Dr. Richards.
First he checked Josh's gums.

Then he used a small mirror
to look for holes called cavities
in Josh's teeth.
He didn't find any cavities.

mirror

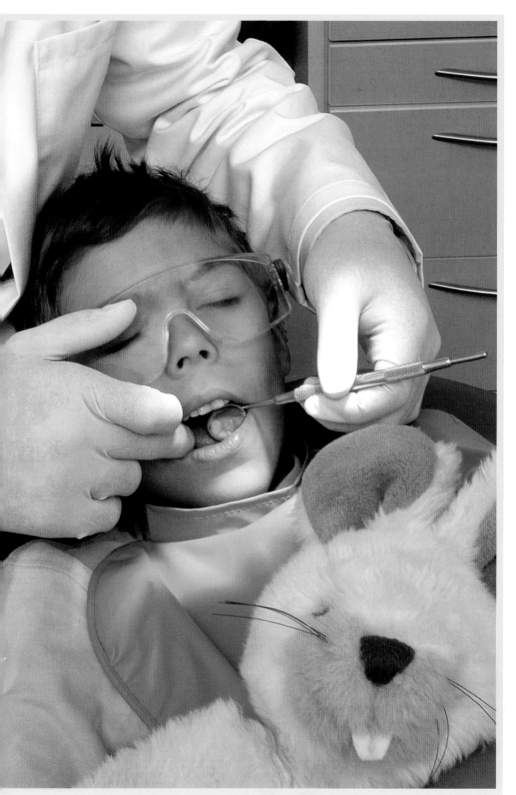

"You need to take extra care
of the molars at the back
of your mouth," he said.
"Right now there is
a sticky layer on them.
This is called plaque.
It can cause cavities,
so you need to
brush it away."

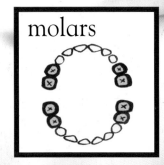

molars

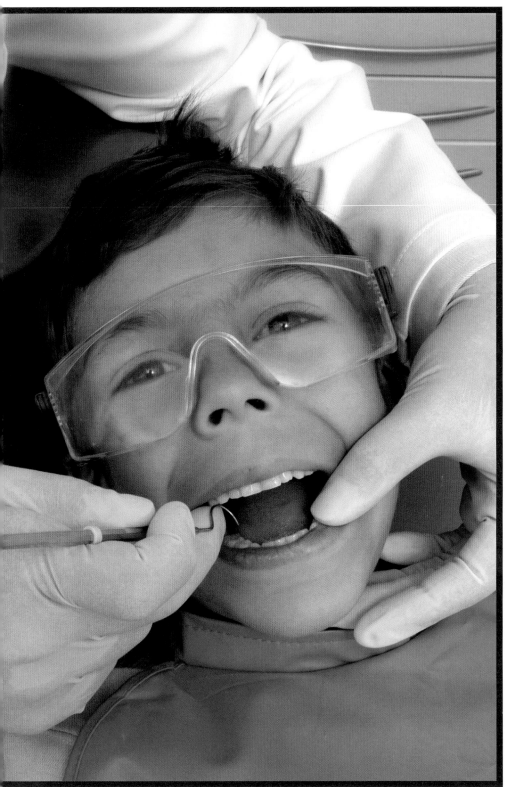

Dr. Richards
showed Josh a good
way to brush.

toothbrush

"Squeeze a pea-sized
blob of toothpaste
onto your toothbrush.
Then gently brush
in little circles," he said.

Josh tried brushing Rabbit's teeth. "How often do you brush your teeth?" asked Dr. Richards.

"Every day, I think," said Josh. "You should brush twice a day, once in the morning and once before you go to bed," said Dr. Richards.

incisors

Then it was
Sarah's turn.
"You've lost six
of your baby teeth,"
said Dr. Richards.

"New incisors are growing at the front. Soon your other baby teeth will get wobbly and fall out. You'll have 32 new teeth in all."

Then Dr. Richards
found a little cavity
in one of Sarah's teeth.

"I'm going to put a
filling here," he said.
"A filling is a kind of
paste that dries hard.
It will keep the cavity
from getting bigger and
giving you a toothache."

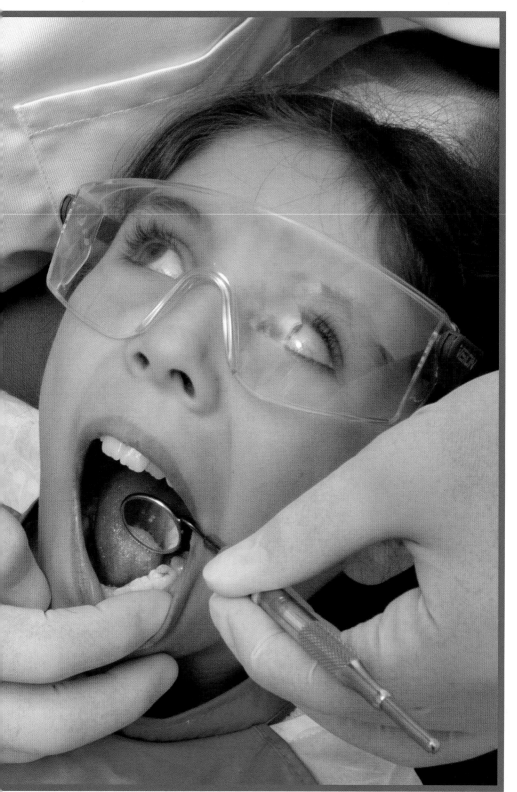

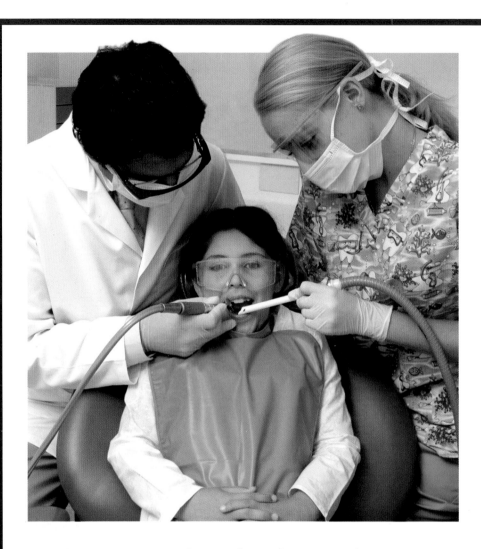

First Dr. Richards cleaned
out the cavity using a drill.
His assistant, Carol, used
a suction tip to suck out
any saliva, or spit.

Then she gave Sarah
a cup of water to
rinse out her mouth.

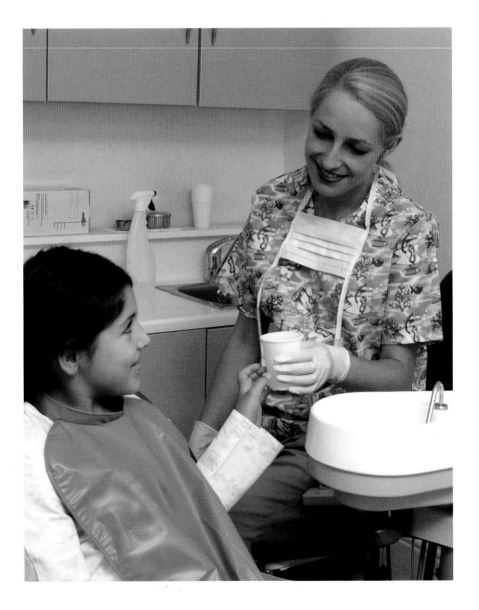

Next Dr. Richards
used an air jet to
blow air into
the cavity.
This dried the
cavity so the
filling would stick.

Then he pushed the filling
neatly into the cavity.
"All done," he said.

Then Dr. Richards
pointed to a chart.
It helped explain how
to prevent cavities.
"Don't have
sugary drinks
or candy very often,
and brush your teeth
twice a day,"
he said.

candy

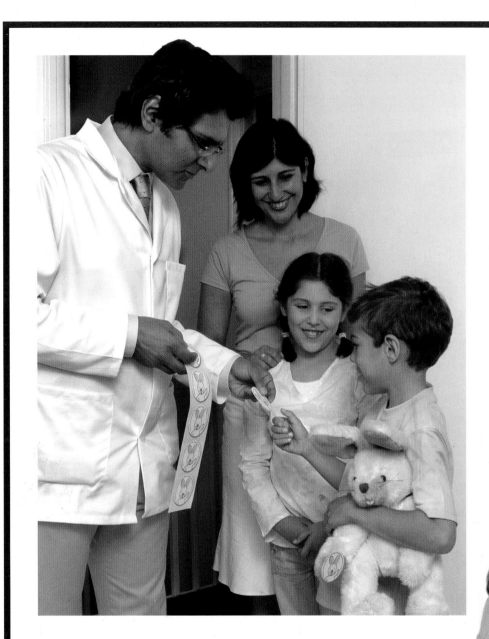

As they were leaving,
Dr. Richards gave Sarah and Josh
each a sticker of a smiling rabbit.

The sticker said,
"To keep your teeth
sparkling clean and bright,
brush early in the morning
and last thing at night."
And that's exactly what
they did!

Picture word list

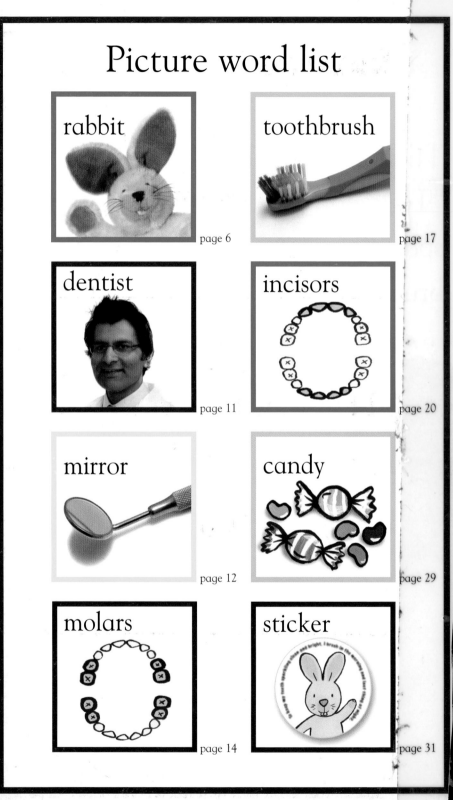

rabbit
page 6

toothbrush
page 17

dentist
page 11

incisors
page 20

mirror
page 12

candy
page 29

molars
page 14

sticker
page 31